Not Available IN Any StorE

For Lucy, laughing
R.R.

For Cindy
S.V.

All rights reserved under International and Pan-American Copyright Conventions. Published in the United States by Pantheon Books, a division of Random House, Inc., New York, and simultaneously in Canada by Random House of Canada Limited, Toronto.

Some of this material has appeared, in slightly altered form, in the *New York Times*, *New England Monthly*, *New York* magazine, and *Lear's*, and on HBO's *Not Necessarily the News*.

Library of Congress Cataloging-in-Publication Data

Rosen, Richard Dean, 1949-
Not available in any store: the complete catalog of the most amazing products never made / by Richard Rosen ; designed and illustrated by Steve Vance.
   p. cm.
 ISB N 0-679-73068-0
 1. Inventions—Humor. 2. Consumers—Humor. I. Title.
PN6231 . I67R6 1990
818'.5407—dc20   90-52513

Manufactured in the United States of America

First Edition

The Complete Catalog of the Most AMAZING Products Never Made!

Not Available IN Any Store

By **RICHARD ROSEN**

Designed and Illustrated by **STEVE VANCE**

Pantheon Books • New York

Contents

CAREER FACILITATORS

LEISURE AND CREATIVITY AIDS

INDEX

Introduction

ONE GLANCE at the state of life on this planet reveals that the consumer culture has been shockingly inattentive to our deepest needs and desires. We have hundreds of products we have no genuine use for, but just try to find something you *really* need. Like a watch that keeps quality time. Or a product that allows you to experience an intimate relationship with no emotional cost to yourself.

Perhaps you've been looking for a cure for a friend's annoying self-promotion. Or a device that allows you to edit out painful memories and experiences. Or a shoe that's right for all the exercise you're not getting.

You've come to the right place. I've traveled far and wide to find products—and some services as well—to help us circumvent all the emotional, practical, and existential complexities that plague our lives.

You know, people like to say things like "Life is compromise" and "You can't have everything." I don't look at it that way. I sincerely feel that we're all entitled to be novelists without writing a single word, to include plenty of bran in our diets without actually eating any, and to undergo successful psychotherapy without having to show up week after week, and to hire specialists to make our small talk for us.

So feel free to browse through the following pages and enter a world of unimagined convenience.

I personally guarantee that if you're not satisfied with any product or service offered in *Not Available in Any Store,* I will promptly refund your money or replace the item. I also guarantee that if you can find any of the products advertised here for a lower price, just send me proof and I'll be glad to send you that product free!

I'd like to thank Diane McWhorter, Lee Aitken, Duncan Darrow, Thomas Friedman, Andrew Kopkind, and Larry Rosen for helping to bring some of these products to my attention. I'm grateful to Daniel Okrent, Peter Herbst, and particularly Robert Lescher, for helping to bring these products to market. And thanks to Susan Orlean for providing this book's title. And my gratitude, finally, to Steve Vance for his literary contributions as well as his artwork.

Richard Rosen
c/o Pantheon Books
201 E.50th St.
New York, N.Y. 10022

A NOTE TO OUR READERS

Have you come across any new products and services that you think warrant inclusion in the next edition of *Not Available in Any Store*? As thorough as our research department is, some things inevitably get through our nets. If you think you've landed a good one, send a description to the above address. If we include it in the next edition, we'll pay you a finder's fee.

Interpersonal Activity Enhancers

IS LONELINESS ANY REASON TO EAT ALONE TONIGHT?

With Chez Vous Video's "Dinner Party Minus One," you can turn your lonely nights into festive, dollar-saving social gatherings.

All you do is insert the three-hour "Dinner Party Minus One" video in your VCR, then place the TV monitor facing you on the dining room table. For the first half-hour, you finish preparing your dinner while ten attractive, professionally trained actors playing your good friends sip cocktails, talk casually among themselves, and occasionally call out to you in the kitchen to ask, "How's every little thing coming?"

Once you've sat down with your meal, the image before you on the monitor shows your guests seated on either side of a long dining table, and all in realistic perspective. Just imagine! Ten "best friends" to keep you company with their clever, professionally scripted conversation, complete with timely gaps for *your* remarks.

Unlike real dinner parties, this one will hardly cost you anything, since yours is the only mouth you have to feed.

And unlike real dinner parties, all of your friends are articulate, well-mannered, scintillating, *positive* people. They're interested, above all, in YOU! They'll ask you about your job, your family, your social life, even your innermost thoughts, and then "listen attentively" while you exercise the Host Speaking Options built right into your "Dinner Party Minus One" tape. You'll be praised on your appearance, your cooking, and your apartment or home. And if you happen to be a glutton for flattery, you're free to rewind the tape and listen to the compliments all over again!

PLUS...Your "Dinner Party Minus One" video can be ordered with customized features designed to make your evening complete. Here are just a couple of suggestions:

•Have one of your guests (please designate male or female) "lean over" and confide how much he or she has always had a crush on you

•Or how about capping your evening with a spontaneous and sincere toast from *all* your friends?

And Chez Vous Video is now offering its "Dinner Party Minus One" in a wide selection of social milieus, including "Literary Salon," "Celibate Singles," and "Couples Only."

So how about it? Turn a lonely meal into a feast of friendship.

And remember—when your "Dinner Party Minus One" ends, the only dishes you'll have to wash are...your own!

DINNER PARTY MINUS ONE
from Chez Vous Video

A FRIEND ON TAPE IS A FRIEND INDEED

YOU LOOK LIKE YOU'VE GOT A LOT ON YOUR MIND-- WHY DON'T YOU TELL ME ABOUT IT?

Sometimes you just don't want a houseful of people. Admit it—what you could use is a good, long heart-to-heart with your very best friend.

Except you don't have a best friend. Maybe you don't have any friends at all.

When certain things are troubling you, let Chez Vous Video lend you a sympathetic ear. The "Tête-à-Tête" Tape provides three full hours of caring conversation with your "best friend," played by an actor with years of experience in Off-Broadway roles as a sensitive contemporary.

Every "Tête-à-Tête" Best Friend listens carefully to your problems, nodding continually, then comforts you at regular intervals with, "I know exactly how you feel," or an empathetic grunt. Your "Tête-à-Tête" Best Friend occasionally will share a personal anecdote that seems oddly relevant, but otherwise the stage is all yours. And at three hours in length, it gives you plenty of time to exhaust even the most obsessive monologues about life's disappointments.

No matter how confused, inarticulate, or clinically depressed you may be, the "Tête-à-Tête" tape "understands" precisely what you mean. And your "Tête-à-Tête" Best Friends never have to excuse themselves to freshen their drinks or go to the bathroom, so you won't lose a moment of sweet confession.

LOVE IS *Lovelier*

THE FIRST TIME AROUND

...thanks to the VENUS 360b RELATIONSHIP SIMULATOR

If you're afraid of intimate relationships, perhaps you'd like to know what you're getting into before you get into it.

By training on the Venus 360b Relationship Simulator, you'll be exposed to all the stages of a love relationship without running the risk of hurting yourself or another person. The Venus 360b Relationship Simulator operates on the same principle as the flight simulators used by professional pilots. In its controlled environment the inexperienced lover can run the entire course of a passionate involvement in a matter of hours.

From the moment you enter the Venus 360b Relationship Simulator compartment to the moment you leave, you'll feel every tenderness and twinge. You'll run the gamut from passion to petulance, from randiness to revulsion.

Each sensation has been digitally reproduced and enhanced to prepare you for actual mating adventures. Once you know what to expect from love, you'll be able to make an intelligent decision about whether getting involved with other people makes any sense at all.

And if you decide that relationships are not for you, you'll know exactly what you're not missing.

For the hands-off experience of romance

The VENUS 360b RELATIONSHIP SIMULATOR faithfully recreates the emotions associated with every phase of deep interpersonal caring:
* **Love at first sight**
* **Vertigo**
* **Infatuation**
* **Approach-avoidance behavior**
* **Deep kissing**
* **Loss of appetite**
* **Consummation**
* **Exchange of family backgrounds, dreams, and fears**
* **Intense predawn conversations**
* **Submersion of ego in the other**
* **Neurotic acting out**
* **Realization of separateness**
* **First intimations of loneliness**
* **"Rediscovery" of love object**
* **First intimations of boredom**
* **More neurotic acting out**
* **Onset of boredom**
* **Mild sexual dysfunction**
* **Still more neurotic acting out**
* **Denial of inevitability of breakup**
* **Transient renewal of interest**
* **Acceptance of breakup**
* **Agonizing predawn conversations**
* **Denial of acceptance of breakup**
* **Acceptance of denial of breakup**
* **Acceptance of denial of acceptance of breakup**
* **Endless recriminations**
* **Prolonged destructive breakup**
* **Redistribution of record collection**
* **Hatefulness**
* **Heartache**
* **Phone calls**
* **Bad-mouthing of ex to others**
* **Manipulation of third parties to effect reconciliation**
* **Resignation**
* **Suicidal ideation**
* **More phone calls**

The **Venus**
360b RELATIONSHIP SIMULATOR
"If love were any more real, you might never recover"

The Call-Waiting Syndrome

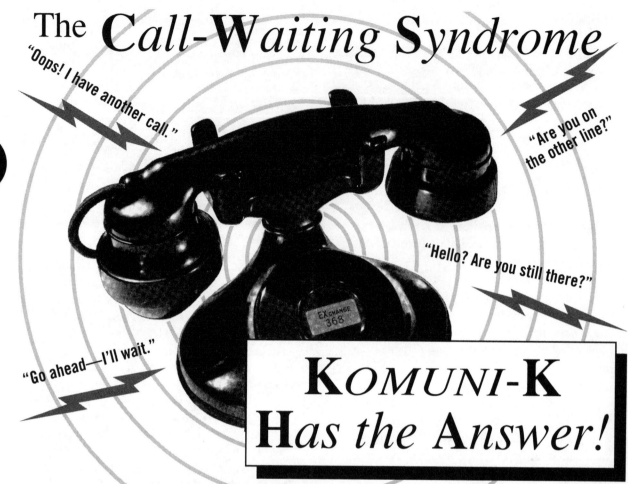

"Oops! I have another call."

"Are you on the other line?"

"Hello? Are you still there?"

"Go ahead—I'll wait."

KOMUNI-K Has the Answer!

YOU KNOW how nervous call-waiting makes you. That insidious beep. The anxiety of having to interrupt a phone conversation to take that second call. The anguish of telling the second caller that you've got someone else on the line. Or the trauma of deciding to take that second call and having to inform the first caller that you have to take the second call and will call back later.

And it's no better being the caller. That paranoid sense that the other person is already on another call when he picks up. The hurt feelings. The deferential, "That's all right, I'll call back." The frenzied response, "No, no, let me get rid of this other call. Stick with me a second." The overwhelming guilt you feel that the other caller isn't as important as you.

Really, it's enough to make you want to send a letter.

But now KOMUNI-K has developed the Second-Call Silencer, a novel device that, once it's attached to your phone base, disarms your Call-Waiting immediately and *prevents any second caller from getting through!*

Think about it—**only one call at a time.** If anyone else tries to get through to you, they'll hear a pleasant "busy" signal, indicating that they should try you later. And you won't even know that someone else was trying to get hold of you. You're free to talk without fear of untimely intrusions or messy "second-caller protocol"!

An idea this revolutionary could come only from the people at KOMUNI-K!

A WORD FROM THE WISE

Dear Not Available:

Can't thank you enough for the Komuni-K Second-Call Silencer. It's just about saved my mental health. Almost all my friends had call-waiting, and when I called them, they'd always be on another call, but they'd tell me they wanted to talk to me and to hold on a second while they dumped their other call. But I never believed they really wanted to talk to me. You know, I just thought they were being nice and didn't want to hurt my feelings because they know how sensitive I am, and I felt bad because I didn't want them to make an exception in my case. I was always certain that the call they were already on was really more important and we'd start arguing. I'd try to convince my friend to take the other call and he'd be saying, "But I want to talk to you," and I'd say, "No, listen, it's nothing important, I'll talk to you later," and they'd say, "Look, if I didn't want to take your call, I wouldn't say so," and I'd say, "It's probably an important business conversation you're having," and they'd say, "No it's not, it's my mother, and I'm glad to have an excuse to get rid of her," and I'd say, "You're just saying that," and I'd end up losing a friend. It was horrible. So I gave my few remaining friends the Second-Call Silencer for Christmas, and as a result, when I call them now I get a busy signal, and I just know they're on a more important call, and there're no arguments about it.

I know you won't publish such an unimportant letter because you've undoubtedly got so many more important ones that you'll want to publish, but I still wanted to express my appreciation for this remarkable device, not that my appreciation counts for anything. I'm aware that you have many more important customers than me.

Robbie Kelk
Clayton, Missouri

THE SECOND-CALL SILENCER
only from

From Pariah to Party Favorite...

...as quick as you can say "MUTE-ME!"

In social situations, do you have an uncontrollable urge to impress others? When it comes to blowing your own horn, are you usually one toot over the line? Do you kick yourself after parties for having told a complete stranger about that award you received, particularly since it had to be forced into a conversation about *his* recent promotion? Does the memory of your gratuitous name-dropping keep you up at night?

Let's face it—sometimes your built-in "censor" just can't do the job and you begin to wonder if you've joined the dreaded company of...People Who Say Too Much.

Now there's a product that provides quick relief from your own vanity.

It's the Electronic Mute-Me, a lightweight device that attaches easily and comfortably over your mouth. Once in place, the Electronic Mute-Me's advanced microchip identifies potentially boastful remarks before you utter them, prefiltering all self-referencing, leaving your verbal output delightfully free of bombast.

In conversation, never again will you:

—Insert the names of posh resorts, especially Caribbean islands with no "native problem"

—Refer to sums of money in terms of five-, six-, and seven-figures

—Mention public figures by their first names

—Use the word "arrondissement" in conversation with someone who's recently been in Paris

It would otherwise take years to accomplish what the Electronic Mute-Me can do the moment you fasten the Velcro harness over your face. Why wait until your reputation as a self-centered boor has grown too great to repair? In the time it once took you to tell total strangers, "I'm very good at what I do," you can now remove all traces of self-absorption from your casual speech.

The Electronic MUTE-ME

BEFORE LOVE TURNS TO HATE, TURN TO US

SOONER OR LATER, it happens in every relationship. One of you thinks you're growing apart, the other doesn't. It's a recipe for serious interpersonal conflict, often with no hope of resolution.

But if you had a way to calculate *objectively* how far apart you'd grown, at least you could agree on one thing. And that would be a start.

The Emotional Distance Estimator from Qualico tells you at the push of a button exactly how emotionally alienated you and

your loved one are. Using ultrasonic sensors, it measures that distance in *disaffectimes*, the international standard of measurement for emotional distance.

Just point the Emotional Distance Estimator at your loved one and press. Instantaneously you'll know, for instance, whether you're 0 *disaffectimes* apart (unhealthy bonding and lack of individuation), 10 *disaffectimes* apart (optimal mix of intimacy and healthy separation) or 25 *disaffectimes* apart (the

point at which negative emotional regard exceeds positive attraction, resulting in irreversible romantic deficit).

Now you can cut all the cackle and get right to the truth about how far apart you've grown. Let the Emotional Distance Estimator tell you once and for all whether it's time for a sincere reevaluation of your involvement, for couple's therapy, or for just getting the hell out of the relationship.

THE EMOTIONAL DISTANCE ESTIMATOR
ONLY FROM QUALICO

The people who bring you the Quatch, the watch that tells quality time, now bring you the only reliable professional protection for quality relationships.

Therapy Got You DOWN?

Everybody knows there are days when you just don't feel like keeping your shrink appointment. Perhaps you're close to a painful insight and simply want to avoid it a little longer. Or you've been stuck on the same issue for months and can't bear to go over it for the twentieth time. Maybe it's raining and you're just too depressed. In any case, you've got better things to do than worry about intrapsychic conflict.

If you only didn't feel so guilty about it.

Now Shrink Mates allows you to skip your session with a clear conscience. Because Shrink Mates is the service that sends a stand-in to your therapist for you. And not just anybody, because Shrink Mates will match you with one of our over 500 trained surrogate neurotics.

Following a short phone interview covering your childhood, your love life, your fears, phobias, fantasies, and obsessions, we'll assign you a compatible Shrink Mate. Then you just let us know when you're not going to be showing up and your shrink will receive a patient of your same sex, age, temperament, and diagnostic category.

Of course, it won't exactly be the same as having you there, but you'll feel better knowing that your shrink won't be spending your hour alone, won't you?

So think of Shrink Mates the next time you feel you'll lose your mind if you hear your therapist say one more time, "What do you think?"

Shrink Mates. Since you're paying for the hour anyway, why not make your therapist work for it?

READ WHAT THESE SATISFIED PATIENTS HAVE TO SAY:

"My Shrink Mate is a godsend. After using her a couple of times, I realized that I enjoyed not showing up at my shrink's so much that now I let my Shrink Mate fill in for me all the time! Sure, it costs me a little more than psychotherapy alone, but I've never felt better in my life!"

Margot Pinieles
Davis, Pennsylvania

"I used my Shrink Mate for a few sessions when I knew my therapist wanted to delve into the reasons for my promiscuity. Believe me, I was not real gung-ho about that. When I returned to therapy, he didn't even know I hadn't been there! That's how good Shrink Mates is. And I'm still as promiscuous as ever! I can heartily recommend Shrink Mates to anyone who's serious about not getting to the bottom of things."

James Meele
Tampa, Florida

"You're not going to believe this, but I was at a club recently and I started talking to this guy who seemed very familiar, and when I asked him what he did for a living, he explained that he was a surrogate therapy patient. Well, it turned out he was my Shrink Mate! What an amazing coincidence. We ended up comparing notes on my—I mean our!—shrink, and that was pretty therapeutic right there. It's great. Now we're friends."

Paul Ustevitch
Chicago, Illinois

SHRINKMATES

"THE BEST THERAPY FOR TOO MUCH THERAPY"

Is this <u>you</u> at parties?

"I, er, you know..."
"Well, uh, well..."
"Gee, uh..."
"Hmmm..."

C'mon, be honest. Is this you? Are you ill-at-ease? Ineffectual?

At last! There is an answer!

What would you say if we told you that there was a simple, easy way to master troubling social circumstances?

It's your own SmallTalk Agent—that's right, a personal agent to stand by your side and represent you at any social gathering. With your own SmallTalk Agent, a charmingly glib professional, you don't have to be at a loss for trivial or incidental conversation, because your SmallTalk Agent will provide it for you.

Prepared for any situation!

Unable to disentangle yourself from a boozy boor? Your SmallTalk Agent will take the abuse for you, then tell him where to get off!

Embarrassed by encounters with enemies you didn't know had also been invited? Every SmallTalk Agent has a repertoire of trenchant insults to put you back on the offensive!

Fearful about approaching that attractive man or woman across the room? Your SmallTalk Agent will not only arrange that first date, but lie convincingly about your present income and educational background!

All this—and so much more!

In addition, our agents are trained to perform all the socially desirable gestures—including the suave laugh, the "power gaze," and the playful slug-on-the-arm—that, were you capable of them yourself, would long ago have made you a successful individual.

Turn that deficit of dazzle into a surplus of style. Our SmallTalk Agents are available by the cocktail hour, or on weekly retainer.

When it comes to human intercourse, why not leave the dirty work to us?

ANOTHER EXAMPLE OF WHY NO "NOT AVAILABLE IN ANY STORE" PRODUCT EVER GROWS OLD!

Thanks to our customers' helpful letters, we've given all our SmallTalk Agents supplementary training so that they can now handle new awkward social situations that have arisen due to recent cultural and political developments. Our agents are now equipped to:

1) Represent you in light conversation about the end of the Cold War. Our agents are briefed monthly on changes in Soviet foreign policy and the vagaries of Communist Party rule in Eastern European (formerly Eastern Bloc) countries. All our agents know a smattering of obscure Russian words designed to intimidate those who try to threaten you with their pretentious grasp of the language.

2) Argue convincingly that the Democratic Party can and will be rehabilitated.

3) Chat knowledgeably about HDL, LDL and triglycerides.

4) Toss off clever pronouncements about the nineties, including predictions about the emerging *zeitgeist*.

No talk's too small for...

Just landed a 5-picture deal

Received a fellowship

Tripled our billing

Seven-figure jury award

Made the *Times* bestseller list

Daughter's at the top of her pre-school class

Don't Let Other People's Good Fortune Ruin Your Day

WE'RE ALL familiar with the situation. You're not feeling that great about yourself when, suddenly, you're exposed to someone else's good fortune, success, or—maybe worst of all—sheer talent.

Announcing revolutionary new protection for the insecure: Lunaka Envyblock.

This is the first lotion that actually blocks the harmful rays emanating from other people's advantages and accomplishments. Lunaka is strong and effective enough to protect you from the especially toxic effects of people who are undeservedly successful, yet gentle enough for daily use by the most pathologically sensitive and jealous individuals. Lunaka Envyblock comes in several formulas, ranging from Number 5, which defends you from only the most damaging assaults on your self-esteem, to Number 15, which works against even the vaguest sense of someone else's superiority and will completely neutralize even the most random encounter with an overachiever.

With Lunaka Envyblock, now you can go to job interviews, counseling sessions, parties, or business meetings and *never* have to worry about your own limitations.

Lunaka Envyblock leaves you at the end of every social contact with a clean, fresh, competent feeling.

Really, why should other people's egos be your problem?

Lunaka ENVYBLOCK

LOTION OR SPRAY

Fight Sleaze SCIENTIFICALLY!

F OR THOUSANDS of people, the Electronic Sleaze Collar has succeeded where confrontation, complaining, and cajoling have failed.

The Electronic Sleaze Collar permanently drives away sleazes with PMBC (pulsed, modulated, burst circuit) sound, a safe, high-frequency sound pitched well beyond animal and human range and audible only to sleazes, slimeballs, and jerks.

In most cases obscene phone callers, time-share resort condominium salesmen, and the majority of show business people die within seconds of being exposed to the transmit-ter's PMBC output...never to annoy you or others again. *There is no other way* to safely and permanently remove idiots from your life. And our new long-life lithium camera battery (with push-to-test LED to show battery is working) means you can exterminate more unbearable people than ever without any special effort on your part.

Remember—only sleazes, slimeballs, shmucks, and ass-holes are destroyed by the Electronic Sleaze Collar. *It will not harm decent people.*

Unless, of course, they begin to act up.

NOTHING WORKS BETTER... 92 PERCENT OF THE TIME.

Since we introduced the Electronic Sleaze Collar to our customers six years ago, it has generated more mail than any other product. Most of the letters have praised this amazing device. However, in about 8 percent of the cases, the Elec-tronic Sleaze Collar does not work. In these cases, the intended victim is not only unaffected, but becomes even more impossible. While we are continuing to test the Electronic Sleaze Collar in our own laboratory, we feel that this paradoxical effect may occur when the wearer himself is a slimeball. To insure your collar's effectiveness we recommend you make sure you're not a shit before making your purchase.

Electronic SLEAZE COLLAR

MR. AND MRS. AMERICA...
YOU NEED

Are you the kind of person who has only a collection of namby-pamby literary allusions to show for all your years of higher education? Has the technology boom caught you with your conversational pants down?

Then you need Verbo-Creations. At Verbo-Creations, a division of Verbonics, we create personalized jargon stylings to facilitate all of your small-talk needs.

CUSTOM-DESIGNED FOR YOUR CONVERSATIONAL REQUIREMENTS

How do we do it? By providing you with Speech Enhancers, those incomprehensible phrases that make you sound as if you're in a very important line of work. We're the oldest company specializing in the polysyllabicization of verbal representations. So no matter how inarticulate or personally unimpressive you may be, we'll devise communication obfuscators that are just right for you.

The next time someone tells you he's developing a femto-second laser apparatus with a four-

Just imagine yourself at your next cocktail party, wandering from guest to guest, dropping bon mots like this:

> That may be, but I'm doubtful whether your statement would bear up under a normal standardization suction-analysis.

> Yes, that's quite common—we call it iatrogenic tiling phenomenon. I'm surprised you haven't heard of it.

> I couldn't help overhearing what you said. As it happens, I've done quite a bit of work myself in the private sector with permanence-inhibitor sleeves.

stage pulse amplification section, you'll be able to shoot back, "Well, I hope you've accounted for the slab saturation effect."

And that's just one of the many incomprehensible terms you can obtain from Verbo-Creations. We'll also teach you how to pronounce and properly integrate such phrases as intensity-sensitive conversion, concept lens, liquefaction phase lift, and negative decathexis ladder.

IMPRESS YOUR FRIENDS—FOOL YOUR FOES

What do these terms mean? Hell if we know! But who cares? Once Verbo-Creations has helped you realize your vernacular potentialities, you'll convince everyone within earshot that you're on the cutting edge of CAD/CAM, interferon research, orthomolecular psychiatry—you name it! Interlocutors will cringe at the range and depth of your knowledge, swoon at your perspicacity! With Verbo-Creations, you're instantly au courant!

Send for your Verbo-Creations proto-prospectus brochure element today! Don't wait another minute to improve your vocation profile aspect and your socialization discretion quotient. You need never suffer from a terminology deficiency posture again!

We're Verbo-Creations.

VerboCreations *From* **VERBONICS**

Life-Management Accessories

At last, a fully electronic component that adapts state-of-the-art digital videotape editing technology to your own life.

Because the Caswell Life-Editing System *interfaces directly with your own memory*, now you can finally control almost everything you think about (and that's the next best thing to controlling reality, isn't it?). At last, you can "call up" unpleasant memories and sensations and "snip" them out of your life. Leave everything from specific recollections to entire periods of your life—early childhood, puberty, the collapse of the bond market, even your first marriage—on "the cutting room floor." Does the mere thought of certain people enrage you? With the Caswell Life-Editing System, you can get them out of your life—forever.

The Caswell Life-Editing System not only removes offending material from your memory, but automatically "splices" your life back together for a seamless and superior version of personal reality. No flash frames. No glitches. And, most of all, no regrets. By erasing bad memories you can say goodbye to guilt once and for all.

And that's only the beginning. Because our playback feature permits you to "relive" your *favorite* moments with remarkable fidelity. You can even access forgotten "unconscious" memories and review them without losing even a generation of clarity.

And it's superior to the original, because our standard digital features allow you to freeze-frame and slo-mo on your most cherished experiences. Who wouldn't like to re-experience that first taste of California sushi roll, that first Mercedes test-drive, that first delicious merger deal, with absolutely no loss of intensity or color vibrancy? By assigning actual SMPTE time code reference numbers to your memory-events, the Caswell Life-Editing System permits you to pinpoint virtual nanoseconds of the pleasurable past!

And our special picture-in-picture function gives you the option of reliving *two* glorious moments at once. That means you can mix-and-match memories for optimum enjoyment. For example, now you can combine a peak romantic experience *and* a career promotion and double your delight! (Who says life isn't better the second time around?) And, of course, our standard built-in digital video effects capability—everything from squeeze wipes to swish pans—will enhance the pleasure of any remembering you choose to do.

The Caswell Life-Editing System—get yours today for a happier yesterday!

Are some of your memories too painful to even review for editing? Our special Auto-Delete feature will remove them for you. Simply punch in the parameters ("Grad School—Mary R.," for instance), and we'll do the rest!

Our exclusive Cin-O-Matic® Edit Control and flying erase head enable you to create fades, wipes, dissolves, and other special effects not normally available outside of expensive optical houses!

Want to linger over an especially gratifying moment? Our MemoRepeat Loop Creator lets you view it over and over at the press of a single button!

31

The *Caswell*

LIFE-EDITING SYSTEM

THE LAW IS ON <u>YOUR</u> SIDE
...when you've got the POCKET LAWYER

ARE YOU TIRED OF HUGE LEGAL BILLS?

In an increasingly litigious world, you never know when you're going to need a lawyer. But the one thing you always know is that it's going to cost you an arm and a leg.

Which is why we know you'll be willing to take the stand in defense of the Lipkin Worthy Buxbaum Valdez Pocket Lawyer. It's the hand-held legal computer so versatile it actually:

- **files nuisance suits**
- **executes lengthy contracts**
- **performs litigation research**
- **answers interrogatories**
- **files motions to compel**
- **makes intimidating phone calls**
- **represents you in all court proceedings**
- **and much more!**

Yes, one powerful integrated system, designed by the prestigious law firm of Lipkin Worthy Buxbaum Valdez, does it all. Now everyone can have access to competent, inexpensive legal counsel. At a cost of less than a thousand dollars, the Lipkin Worthy Buxbaum Valdez Pocket Lawyer **pays for itself in only *six hours of use.***

Just think of the savings if you're up on a murder charge.

The Lipkin Worthy Buxbaum Valdez Pocket Lawyer is one product you can trust because it's got the Lipkin Worthy Buxbaum Valdez name on it.

And best of all...it never, *ever* sends you a bill.

That's the whole truth, and nothing but.

WE OWE YOU ONE, PAT

Dear Not Available in Any Store:
   When I was arrested for armed robbery almost three years ago, I was stupid enough to use the Lipkin Worthy Buxbaum Valdez Pocket Lawyer to defend myself. Not only did it forget to call two key alibi witnesses, but it short-circuited during its closing argument and identified me as the robber. Then I couldn't get it to file an appeal on my behalf (the repairman said it was a hard-disk problem) and it's never visited me once in prison.
   So you can go screw yourself with your Pocket Lawyer. I'm doing eight years because of it, and when I'm out I'm coming to see you first, buddy.

   Patrick Wheeler
   Rahway, New Jersey

Dear Pat:
   I'd like to thank you for bringing some of the Pocket Lawyer's flaws to our attention. I'm sending you a new one, which I trust you'll find useful in your efforts to win a retrial.
   By the way, Pat, you're not the first Pocket Lawyer customer to complain. A woman in Florida lost custody of her two children to her alcoholic husband when she pushed the wrong function key in court and her Pocket Lawyer accused her of having been a prostitute in Pensacola for several years. She had, in fact, never stepped foot in Pensacola, but the jury believed the Pocket Lawyer.
   In any case, the Pocket Lawyer I'm sending you is an improved model and we are continuing to perfect the product. I'm sure that by the time you're out of prison, its inadvertent tendency to turn on its clients will have been corrected.

   Thanks for your patience,
   Richard Rosen

33

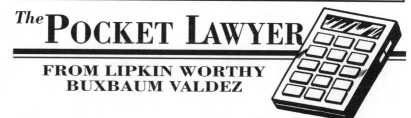

The **POCKET LAWYER**
FROM LIPKIN WORTHY BUXBAUM VALDEZ

NO MORE GUILTY MOMMY!

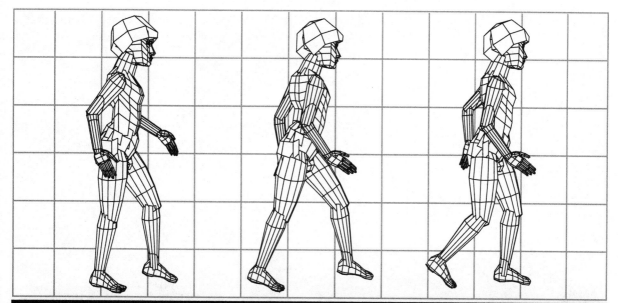

Using 3-D video analysis and our own computerized KinAesthetic Modeling (similar to the technique used for expensive golf lessons), we program your FacsiMommy to match your walk, your posture, even the subtle nuances of your body language!

DO YOU FEEL a little guilty every morning when you leave your child with its nanny or at the day care center on your way to work?

It's only human.

Now Drill Laboratories has found a way to take the ambivalence out of ambition. Now you can go for that promotion *without* all that emotional commotion. Now you can pursue your career and no one sheds a tear.

No, it's not exactly Mommy...it's FacsiMommy!

Yes, a realistic life-size model of Mommy—dressed in Mommy's clothes and wearing Mommy's "smell." Your child need never be far from a calming representation of his or her maternal caregiver. What's more, at the flick of a switch, a built-in audiocassette player delivers some of Mommy's favorite prerecorded messages. So while you're downtown at the dictaphone, you can still console your child thanks to FacsiMommy's realistic working mouth.

And FacsiMommy is so lifelike that many children can't even tell the difference!

All you have to do is visit a Drill Laboratories FacsiMommy Center and we'll measure you and make a facial mold. In no time, you'll be among the growing number of women who realize that two Mommies *are* better than one. Especially when one's a FacsiMommy!

Don't let your children say that you were never "there" for them.

THEY'LL NEVER KNOW IT'S...
FACSIMOMMY

Be Sure
Your Grief Is
Good
Grief

Grief is one of the most difficult human emotions to endure. Ask anyone who's trying to recover from the loss of a loved one or the end of an important relationship.

According to the experts, you can expect to pass through several phases of grief, including the stages of denial, acceptance, anger, and resignation. But it's not so easy remembering their proper order, or knowing when it's time to move from one stage to the other. As if you didn't feel bad enough as it is.

When mourning threatens to disrupt your normal schedule, let the Gladstone Grief Processor do the work for you. Now you can cut the length of your mourning period up to 95 percent by electronically condensing the neuropsychological process by which you assimilate loss and "get on with your life."

As soon as you attach the electrodes to your temples, signals on the liquid crystal display screen begin to guide you painlessly through the stages of grief, enabling you to radically abbreviate the process through simple biofeedback techniques. A depth discriminator lets you know how genuine your sadness is, and a signal-intensity meter monitors your despair for those troubling lapses of mourning adequacy. And because not all grieving is the same, the Gladstone Grief Processor's unique Loss Mode Selector allows you to choose the appropriate setting (Spouse, Parent, Lover, Uncle by Marriage, etc.) to insure the most economical emotional recovery time.

Within a matter of days, you can completely overcome the untimely personal catastrophes that used to require months—even years—of suffering to be worked through. The Gladstone Grief Processor absolutely guarantees that when the screen finally flashes "Congratulations! Mourning Completed," you'll feel rested, renewed...and as if nothing bad had ever happened.

The Gladstone Grief Processor can't bring back the person you've lost, but this extraordinary piece of emotion reduction technology can take the sorrow out of grieving.

THE GLADSTONE
Grief Processor

The *Quatch*

For When You're Keeping Quality Time

B ECAUSE YOU spend so much time thinking about yourself, you only have a few moments to spend with your child or spouse. How can you be sure it's really Quality Time, and not just Regular Time that contains moments of eye contact and sympathetic listening?

When you wear a Quatch from Qualico you'll always know what time it is, because the Quatch's special heat sensors give off a reassuring hum to let you know you're exuding the warmth, intimacy, and intensity that indicate Quality Time. And as soon as the time you're spending falls below Quality Time level, the Quatch beeps gently to remind you that you can do better.

By reinforcing your Quality Time behavior, the Quatch makes it easy for you to achieve—and maintain—the Quality Time that's so important with your busy schedule. And the Quatch's long-life alarm lets you know when your time's up and it's time to return to whatever it is that's so time-consuming that only Quality Time will do for the ones you love.

Remember: Quality Time is that time which, if you are not spending it, causes you to waste more time worrying about it than the time it takes to learn how to spend Quality Time the Quatch way. When you wear a Quatch, you're well on your way to reducing Regular Time to the very essence of interpersonal contact. Eventually, you'll be spending time of such high quality that you'll be able to carry on meaningful, loving relationships without devoting any time to them at all.

THE **QUATCH**
FROM QUALICO

AT THE KAGLE CLINIC, WE PUT THE LOVE BACK IN FAMILY LIFE

Raising kids in today's world can be a harrowing responsibility. Since no two children are alike, inequalities among them naturally arise. Differences in size, age, sex, intelligence, temperament, physical and emotional development—any of these can cause problems ranging from unnecessary and inefficient diversity to family-shattering tension and conflict.

More and more studies show that young people can actually be damaged for life by the inequalities of childhood.

But now there's great news for parents. Now there's a creative alternative to raising kids the old-fashioned way...

SIBLING-EQUALIZATION SURGERY!

THE MODERN SOLUTION TO AN AGE-OLD PROBLEM!

Sibling Equalization Surgery (SES) and follow-up therapy is a proven method for *removing all those traces of individuality in your children that can be the cause of potentially harmful family conflict.*

Advances in genetic engineering and laser neurosurgery have made it possible, at last, to homogenize your offspring.

Quite frankly, this procedure takes the worry out of child-rearing. Imagine: all your children are now *completely alike* and will continue to develop at the *very same rate.* No more playing favorites and feeling guilty about it.

No more fighting at home over who gets to watch which television show. No more pain because one of your children is better at school or more attractive than the others. And once jealousy and competition *between* your children are eliminated, you, as their parent, will be spared their anger and resentment forever. (You'll also be spared those costly psychotherapy bills that can result from family friction.)

At the Kagle Clinic, we pioneered Sibling-Equalization Surgery and its follow-up treatment. Call us for a free initial consultation.

And bring the kids.

READ WHAT THESE SATISFIED PATIENTS HAVE TO SAY:

"THRILLED!"

"...When I first heard about Sibling-Equalization Surgery, I was skeptical. But when I saw the results for our 14-year-old daughter and 6-year-old son, I was thrilled..."

Mrs. H. B., Miami, Florida

"MARVELOUS!"

"We were afraid we were spoiling our youngest daughter, Sally, and alienating our eldest, Ann. But now, thanks to your procedure, we can no longer tell them apart! In fact, we call them both 'Sally Ann'..."

T. L., Rochester, New York

"ADDED BENEFITS"

"...We've experienced many added benefits not mentioned in your brochure, including a dramatic savings of time and money, since we no longer have to shop for three separate wardrobes..."

Mrs. J. S., Chico, California

CAN YOU HAVE TOO MUCH OF A GOOD THING?

What if your offspring were <u>born</u> equal? Does having twins mean you have nothing to worry about? Sadly, the answer is NO! Many doctors agree—<u>too</u> <u>much</u> equality can have a negative effect on your children's well-being—not to mention the wear and tear on you! Coping with one helpless infant at a time is trying enough. That's why we at Kagle are pleased to offer Twin Differentiation Surgery, a simple and effective technique to help you through the arduous task of multiple parenting. Thanks to our newly developed Asynchronous Maturation Process, you can take on the traumas of teething, toilet training, or the "terrible twos" ONE CHILD AT A TIME! Then, once you've navigated the perils of early childhood development, a quick visit to Kagle for Sibling Equalization Surgery brings you the easy-to-handle homogeneity that will be so useful in the turbulent years ahead!

WRITE TODAY FOR OUR FREE CATALOG!

The GENTRIFIER
Don't Find a Home Without It!

MOST OF THE GREAT neighborhoods are already gentrified. So if you're not presently a home- or condo-owner in the urban neighborhood of your choice you already may be wondering if you're not doomed to be a victim of gentrification instead of its beneficiary. Your only hope may lie in becoming a "pioneer"—one of the courageous people who buy early and cheaply in an as yet "undiscovered" neighborhood. Of course, if you're like most people, you're afraid you'll choose the wrong neighborhood and end up living next to a soup kitchen for the rest of your life.

NEW HOME-BUYING BREAKTHROUGH

That's why you need the Gentrifier. From Protique. Of all the gentrification-prediction products on the market, the Gentrifier alone enables you to go into any urban wasteland and confidently determine its actual potential as a fully gentrified environment. Why pay $250,000, $300,000, even as much as a half-million dollars to live in a space whose previous tenant paid $135 a month, when you can be the first on someone else's block to send your kid to the pocket playground with a nanny?

Protique means that now you can pioneer without fear. You can displace without disgrace. You can live where you want and let other people live somewhere else.

Get yourself the Gentrifier today. It's either that or the suburbs.

Here's just a sample of what you get:

•A simple multiple-choice test developed by University of Southern Minnesota psychologists that quickly assesses the tractability of long-term residents. All you do is knock on doors, ask a series of ten questions (printed in phonetic Spanish as well as English), and chart "Resident Resistance" on the Gentrifier's Docility Scale. (Sample question: "How would you respond if you couldn't find an ice cube tray for less than $4 in your neighborhood? A) I'd boost one B) I like warm beverages C) I'd move closer to a store that sells cheaper ice cube trays.")

•The patented Protique Loft Locator, a unique sonar device that detects existing large, open interior spaces when pointed at a given building, so you needn't disturb current occupants.

•An audiocassette anthology of soft-rock hits by white performers and black performers pretending to be white. Studies have shown that public response to our specially selected songs, when played at high volume on the street at midnight, is a valuable index of the entrenchment of a community's underclass values, and therefore a guide to the degree of social unrest that a process of gentrification would entail.

•An assortment of token incentives for renters to move out, including cash inducements and lovely trinkets hand-carved by Wellesley graduates.

The GENTRIFIER

YOU DON'T HAVE TO DO IT ALONE

Y OU NEVER THOUGHT it would happen to you. It was always the other guy, wasn't it?

If you have a status-abuse problem, we'd like to help at the Tarpley Center. Acquisitiveness *can* be treated. Come "share" your excesses with us in an atmosphere of privacy, discretion, and moderation.

Compulsive interior decorating? Children named Pemberton or Leland? A home in Spain that you've never used? Whether you're addicted to cocaine, Cozumel, or Corinthian leather, isn't it nice to know there's a place you can go to regain your perspective that's staffed by people who used to be just as shallow as you?

Through a combination of individual and group therapy, plus brute physical force, we'll show you how to recover from the ravages of young urban professionalism and live happily without a vast discretionary income. Our motto is, "One Purchase at a Time." Make it your reality.

You *can* get well.

The Tarpley Center
In Green Bay, Wisconsin

Imagine being dropped by parachute into a totally unfamiliar upper-middle-class suburb with no money and no change of clothes...

Imagine having to survive under these conditions for an entire week, fending for yourself among strange shopping malls and sprawling residential developments inhabited by no one you know personally in either a business or a social context.

Well, that is exactly what Upward Bound offers the seasoned vacationer who's already tested his or her mettle at La Costa or Vail and yearns for a new challenge. Through Upward Bound, even those already acquainted with suburban living find themselves face to face with the unique perils of the bedroom community. Are you resourceful enough to make a frivolous purchase without money, without as much as a credit card? Are you tough enough to walk into the pro shop wearing bellbottoms?

During your Upward Bound week you will learn typical suburban wilderness skills such as lighting a hibachi without using a match and convincing a butcher to deliver despite the fact that you don't have an address. Where will you sleep? Our guides will teach you how to scale mini-stockade fences, foil alarm systems, break into homes when the owners are away, use their beds, and cover all traces of your intrusion before you leave in the morning. You'll also receive expert instruction in tracking the scent of catered parties to forage for leftovers.

But perhaps the greatest challenge awaits those who want to go for the coveted Lawn Boy Award at the end of your Upward Bound week: You will be expected to gain admission to the local

country club, although all country clubs in participating Upward Bound communities have at least a two-year waiting list and don't admit members of your religion. (As if it isn't already enough that you have a weak second serve!)

For the ultimate in thrills, personal growth, and potential future business contacts, make sure your next vacation is Upward Bound!

UPWARD BOUND
Find out who you *really* are!

Upward Bound weeks are available year-round. For a brochure and list of participating suburbs, write Upward Bound, Box 717, Garden Hills, IL 92014.

Don't Wait for Bad News On Your Doorstep

IF YOU'RE RUNNING FOR OFFICE, HERE'S ONE WAY NOT TO FALL ON YOUR FACE

IN A WORLD of shifting values, sometimes it's hard to know whether you're a decent human being. Particularly if you have no ethical principles by which to judge your conduct.

So some of us just go about our business until it's too late and we're running the risk of ostracism, public humiliation, fines, or even jail sentences for actions we just "didn't know" were wrong.

If you're thinking of running for political office or are in line for a highly visible job, wouldn't it be nice if there were a simple way to protect yourself from future fiasco by testing your morality in the privacy of your own home?

There is. It's called the Turpitude Home Testing Kit and it's from your friends at Sugarman Laboratories.

Within moments, the Turpitude Home Testing Kit lets you know whether or not you suffer from moral turpitude and related conditions like malevolence.

The test only takes a few minutes and delivers results that are easy to read, leaving no doubt as to your degree of personal moral corruption.

So "Take the Test." It can save you a lot of heartache. Not to mention saving the country a lot of trouble.

Now you can "Take the Test" and discover:

—Whether you're capable not just of driving while mildly intoxicated, but of driving off the road and into a body of water with a passenger in the car and then leaving the scene of the accident.

—Whether you're capable not just of carrying on a romantic affair while married to a long-suffering wife, but of conducting the affair in plain view, daring reporters to expose it, and inviting photographers to make a visual public record of it.

—Whether you're merely incapable of reporting a restaurant bill error in your favor, or would be willing to abuse your publicly vested power in exchange for large sums of cash.

—Whether you are merely a victim of unorthodox sexual urges, or feel compelled to engage in long-term relationships of a compromising nature while capitalizing on a reputation for being above reproach.

49

The TURPITUDE HOME TESTING KIT

SUGARMAN LABORATORIES

51

UP TO YOUR NECK
IN DRECK?

For years, you've been buying and collecting *tchotchkes*...and now they've taken over the house. A lifetime of trivial, ill-advised, and impulsive purchases has turned your domicile into a den of gewgaws, knickknacks, china dogs, and souvenir menus from Wolfie's.

Oy.

But you'd *plotz* if you had to get rid of a single thing yourself.

We understand. When you're up to your neck in dreck, it's time to call Peltz & Feltfinder, the de-*tchotchke*fication experts. We have over 100 years of bric-a-brac-removal experience. For you, Peltz & Feltfinder comes direct to your house and within a matter of hours turns your home into a *tchotchke*-free environment, making room for objects of real value.

We go right to work. First we appraise a little, then we bag and dispose of all the nothings that have been making you *meshugge* for ages. Before you know it, tabletops, shelves, credenzas, and closets we make nice and *tchotchke*-free. Experts like us you couldn't find anywhere.

Call us—that's Peltz & Feltfinder—when sentiment is the only thing standing between you and discarding a piece of junk.

We don't *potchkeh* around.

PELTZ & FELTFINDER

54

WHAT IF YOU DON'T LIKE BRAN?

NO ONE disputes the importance of bran in the diet. We only wish it tasted better. We'd be satisfied if it just looked better.

BRAN—WITHOUT THE BOTHER!

Now there's good news for the bran-resistant. With the **Spitzer Bran Sac**, you can get *all the bran you need* in your diet *without actually having to eat any!*

NEW MEDICAL BREAKTHROUGH!

Invented by world-famous gastroenterologist Dr. Robert Z. Spitzer, the Spitzer Bran Sac contains a six-month supply of highly concentrated bran. When the tough latex rubber sac is surgically implanted at the entrance to your small intestine in a safe and simple procedure, a tiny computer chip directs it to release a daily dose of bran into your digestive system. At the end of six months, a short visit to your local Bran Sac Center is all it takes to replenish your supply.

It gives you all the fiber, without the fuss.

There's only one thing easier than using the Spitzer Bran Sac. Not eating bran at all. And you wouldn't want that, would you?

SPITZER

Bran Sac

PUT YOUR AIRPLANE FOOD WHERE YOUR MOUTH IS!

PLANE TRAVEL in coach has its drawbacks, but none as frustrating as trying to eat your in-flight meal in close quarters. With so little room to maneuver, conveying your meal to your mouth is an adventure you never bargained for. The food is as likely to end up in your lap or the seat pocket in front of you as in your mouth.

And with food this good you don't want to miss a single bite.

The Aeroflex In-Flight Eating Apparatus provides you with an extra arm designed specifically for coach-class dining endeavors, just to make sure that every tasty bit goes just where you want it to.

The Aeroflex In-Flight Eating Apparatus has a single telescoping lightweight aluminum arm, secured to your rib cage by a quality leather harness and adjustable to the exact distance between the tray table and your mouth. It's spring-loaded, so that once you've used a free hand to place that next appetizing mouthful on the arm's stainless steel utensil, all you have to do is press the release button and that succulent morsel of airline fare is instantly catapulted into your waiting maw.

Mm-mmm...We're at culinary cruising altitude now!

Load and release—that's all there is to it! Now you can enter your entree orally without interference from your fellow passengers. Just make sure you don't move your head or that delicious forkful of boned and reconstituted chicken could end up sixteen rows behind you!

So if you want to enjoy fine cuisine five miles high, it's either the Aeroflex In-Flight Eating Apparatus...or flying first class.

AEROFLEX
IN-FLIGHT EATING APPARATUS

IS YOUR HOME YOUR CASTLE OR NOT?

I N TODAY'S crime-ridden society, an electronic home-security system is not only too costly for most people, but also it no longer affords enough protection. Because your average burglar is smarter than your average intrusion-detection system.

That's why, when their private property's at stake, more and more people are turning to the Harrison Moat. It's the only sensible way to defend your home against the invasive actions of criminals, riffraff, common peasants, and disabled motorists.

At Harrison, we understand that next to your wife, your home is your most treasured possession. When we encircle your property with a Harrison Moat, we are giving you protection in the best medieval tradition. When the drawbridge is up, you're free to sleep the sleep of a feudal lord.

Just think of what you're buying in peace of mind and virtually maintenance-free protection. With a Harrison Moat, there are no noisy alarms, hard-wire or wireless devices, no need for costly intercom systems, electromagnetic door locks, or keyless digital pads.

It's the quiet, effective, *natural* way to make your property truly private.

ASK US ABOUT OUR TURRETS AND BATTLEMENTS!

Because no security system is absolutely 100 percent safe under all circumstances, you'll want to look at our wide selection of Harrison turrets and battlements. Made of durable lightweight Gran-It masonry, our turrets and battlements are easily installed on top of your present home, affording complete protection for your sentries. Crouched behind a Harrison, any sentry will be more confident about annihilating intruders. See our catalog for our full line of crossbows and boiling oils.

Come home to a

Harrison

(Water Not Included)

Make Every Day A Beautiful Day

...with *Stewart*
GOODLIFE LENSES

Poverty's unsightly, and until now you've had no choice but to deal with it, especially in urban areas.

These days there's even more of it, and that means there's more of it you wish would just go away so you can pretend that everyone else is as fortunate as you are.

Look, you can't go through life with your eyes closed. But you can go through life wearing a pair of Stewart Goodlife Lenses. They're the one and only contact lens that filters out poverty and the poor from your field of vision, leaving only pleasing people and objects to contemplate.

Make slums, inner-city debris, and the indigent disappear once and for all. Stewart Goodlife Lenses eliminate from your purview anyone making less than $15,500 a year, anyone on public assistance, even cars more than six years old! Since there's nothing you can do about poverty anyway, why be reminded of it?

And for the economically hypersensitive, try our high-opacity Super Goodlife Lenses, rated at $31,000 a year! Isn't it time you started wearing Goodlife Lenses? Don't let poverty ruin your visual aesthetic.

ANNOUNCING A NEW ACCESORY FOR THE <u>COMPLETE</u> GOOD LIFE

Yes, our Goodlife Lenses work wonders when it comes to preserving and enhancing the serenity of your visual environment. But as many of us have found, sometimes that's just not enough. Even the most fully filtered, pleasingly upscale vista can be disrupted by the sudden intrusion of honking car horns, blaring boom boxes, noisy domestic disputes, and the like. That's why we at Stewart are proud to introduce our NEW E-Z Listener Audio Processor. This tiny, featherweight device fits comfortably behind either ear and, using our exclusive Onboard Sinewave Analysis System, *automatically screens out the annoying sounds of the underclass!* Its ten-position sensitivity control allows you to select the precise amount of sonic obstruction that's right for you. Setting 1 eliminates only the most irritating sounds—rap music, car alarms (E-Z Listener's OSA System can, of course, be programmed to block out all car alarms except *yours*), and the like. Setting 10 removes even the faintest aural traces of the underprivileged.

And if you've ever found yourself facing an ungrateful subordinate at the office or wished you could escape from a tedious fellow guest at a party, you'll want to try our E-Z Listener Super-Sonic model, for the ultimate audio-enhancement experience. It has all the features of our regular model PLUS extra filters designed for social and professional situations AND a sophisticated voice synthesizer that can converse charmingly about any one of more than 600 different subjects. Now you can hear, instead of insolent backtalk or banal chitchat, a witty commentary on current events, receive helpful tips on your golf game, or even get up-to-the-minute market quotations. And, thanks to our unique Response Synchronization System, you'll be cued to nod, smile, or murmur, "umm-hmm" at appropriate intervals, so your inattentiveness to the conversation at hand will be *completely undetectable.*

Goodlife

Lenses and Accesories

FROM STEWART—THEY MAY COST MORE, BUT AREN'T YOU WORTH IT?

Career Facilitators

DARN IT! THAT'S THE THIRD TIME THIS WEEK THAT THE BOSS HAS CAUGHT ME READING THE BOX SCORES INSTEAD OF THE SALES REPORTS! YOU GOOF OFF EVEN MORE THAN I DO, CHERYL, BUT YOU NEVER GET CAUGHT! WHAT'S YOUR SECRET?
IT'S NO SECRET, HAL! IT'S BOSS ALERT!
YOU'RE THE BOSS WITH
BOSS ALERT!
THE Amazing DEVICE THAT WILL HELP YOU TO:
IMPRESS YOUR EMPLOYER!
ENJOY YOUR OCCUPATION!
BE THE ENVY OF YOUR PEERS!

No assembly or installation required! It's as easy as 1-2-3!

1. CONTACT! Simply touch the Sensi-Patch to your employer's skin.

2. CONCEAL! The Boss Alert's design blends in with your desktop decor.

3. CONTROL! The Boss Alert puts you in charge, so you can goof off with impunity!

When you're at work, you can't *always* be doing your job. Sometimes you need to make personal phone calls, file your nails, work on outside projects, or just practice foul-shooting on your Nerf basketball set.

The one thing you don't need is for your boss to catch you doing it.

With Boss Alert there's no chance of that. Boss Alert is a state-of-the-art DEEW (Distant Early Employer Warning) System that lets you know when your boss is within 30

feet, giving you plenty of time to get off the phone or put that Nerf basketball back in your bottom drawer. By the time your boss pokes his head in your office, you're once again a model employee.

Here's how it works. Just furtively rub the Boss Alert's Sensi-Patch against any part of your employer's skin. The Boss Alert "remembers" the unique smell of his or her pheromones.Then place the Boss Alert on your desk and go about your business... even if it's not the business

you're getting paid for! The Boss Alert beeps discreetly to let you know it's time to put your nose back to that grindstone.

The Boss Alert comes in three alluring disguises—Petite Rolodex, Electric Pencil Sharpener, and Small Potted Desk Plant—so your employer never needs to know who's the real boss!

So get Boss Alert. And *don't* get caught napping...or talking to your boy-friend...or playing with your cuticles...

BOSS ALERT

WRITE TODAY FOR OUR FREE BROCHURE!

NOW!
YOU CAN BE A NOVELIST
MY COLLEGE NOVEL
by
YOUR NAME HERE

WITHOUT WRITING A SINGLE WORD!

If you're in your thirties or forties and the graduate of a prestige university, you've probably experienced an overwhelming desire to write a novel about a group of your old college friends and what happened to them. But you just don't have the time, or perhaps the talent, to cash in on this lucrative literary perennial.

AT LAST! SCIENCE HAS THE ANSWER!

Still, wouldn't it be nice to make a personal contribution to the growing body of "college" novels? Well, with a little help from the folks at Noveltron, now you can.

All you do is fill out our detailed questionnaire about your college experience, including updated information on your "small circle of friends," and let our computer go to work. Presto! Within days, we'll prepare a gripping, erotic novel about men and women like you contending with life's choices, chances, and limitations. A novel that bristles with such classic human themes as the loss of innocence, loss of love, and loss of income, the squandering of early promise, the ravages of time, the rocky road to recovery, and many more!

NO MANUSCRIPTS TO TYPE— NO DETAILS TO REMEMBER!

And here's the best news: Even if you *don't know* what happened to your old college friends—even if you never *had* any college friends—there's no need to worry. Noveltron's data bank contains over 100 College Character Types (including the charismatic minority recruit and the secretly gay All-American athlete), over 1200 Life Outcomes (from prosperity to the poorhouse), and countless Period Details (student strike posters, plot synopses from *Star Trek*, and the resignation speech of Richard Nixon). Just give us the name of your college, the year you graduated, and the title of your favorite Hermann Hesse novel, and our computer will be glad to extrapolate a completely plausible, catastrophic plot-line with a best-selling emphasis on bitter divorce, pathetic downward mobility, impotence, breakdown, embezzlement, eating disorders, and addictive behavior. And nothing bad happens to you, the main character...unless you want it to!

Why waste all those valuable college years? Everyone's interested in the highly original story of what became of you and the people you knew "back when."

So if you've got that "one great novel in you," why not let Noveltron write it for you?

PUBLISHERS' RESTRICTION:

If you attended a state university or an institution of higher learning with the words "East" or West" in the name, our computer will automatically replace your low-profile school with a randomly selected Ivy League college.

65

NOVELTRON
OF NEW HAVEN, CONNECTICUT

And For That Sensitive Young Wordsmith...
The PRINCESS NOVELTRON

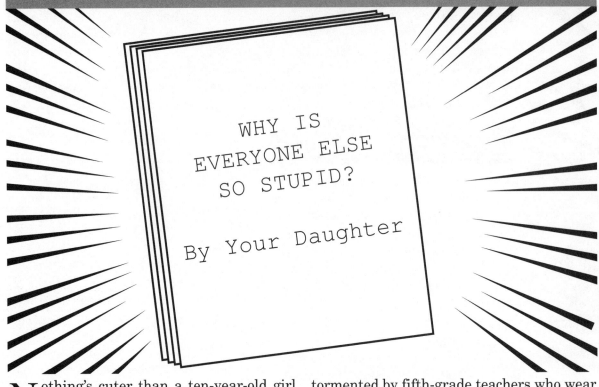

WHY IS
EVERYONE ELSE
SO STUPID?

By Your Daughter

Nothing's cuter than a ten-year-old girl who writes novels. Thanks to Princess Noveltron, now even the dullest daughter can charm her parents with premature literary flair!

Just send us your daughter's name, the names of her best friend, favorite stuffed animal, and grammar school, and we'll send you a fourteen-page "novel" in typewritten manuscript (complete with adorable misspellings) that features your daughter in a variety of preadolescent predicaments: being tormented by fifth-grade teachers who wear stupid clothes, totally misunderstood by dumb siblings, being totally sickened by her dawning awareness of life's stupid unfairness, and basically hating everyone and everything as she all the while keeps tossing her mane of hair and wishing she were completely dead.

Call us now. She may not appreciate it right away, but twenty years from now, won't she be amazed to know that she once had such a rich imagination!

Princess NOVELTRON

JUST BECAUSE YOU'RE NEUROTIC DOESN'T MEAN YOU DON'T NEED TO PLAN AHEAD!

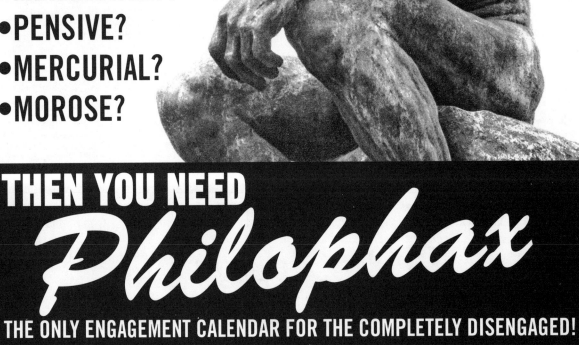

Are You:

- INTROSPECTIVE?
- SELF-ABSORBED?
- BROODING?
- MELANCHOLY?
- PENSIVE?
- MERCURIAL?
- MOROSE?

THEN YOU NEED

Philophax

THE ONLY ENGAGEMENT CALENDAR FOR THE COMPLETELY DISENGAGED!

PHILOPHAX introduces the <u>first</u> <u>complete</u> <u>planning</u> <u>system</u> for people who have no interest in the outer world!

Yes, the Philophax Daily Planner now makes it possible for those too introverted or reclusive to have appointments, meetings, or "things to do" to keep an accurate record of <u>all</u> their mental events!

Every Philophax comes with the following standard daily headings:

- **Anxieties**—make up to five daily entries
- **Regrets**—ample space to record all your missed opportunities and minor guilt
- **Philosophical Quandaries**—make daily notes on all the existential imponderables that plague your consciousness
- **Unrealistic Fantasies**—keep track of all your dreams, no matter how immature
- **Pointless Obsessions**—plenty of room to put down those favorite fixations, even if they remain the same day after day

And to further help you organize your lack of productivity, Philophax provides you with an exclusive Five-Year Fear Planner, a fold-out calendar that lets you record not only your present fears, but the fears you fear that you'll fear far into the future.

You'll also get an Unmade-Phone-Call Log and an Unrealized-Ambition Reminder to torment you with everything you haven't accomplished...and no doubt never will.

And you'll get a Lifetime Dashed-Hopes Memo, so you can see—at a glance—every disappointment you've ever experienced.

Most important, since we know you don't have it together enough even to order a Philophax Daily Planner, we'll send you one immediately and wait for your payment, even if it takes years.

Philophax. It's the only way for the self-absorbed and philosophical to make any sense out of their busy inner lives.

Handsome Binder!
The Philophax is available with your choice of matte black or semi-gloss black cover! Durable finish resists wear, stains, tears! With our easy refill packs, your Philophax will last through years of obsessive auto-analysis!

The **PHILOPHAX** Company
OF ATHENS, GEORGIA

MAKING THE EXAMINED LIFE MORE WORTH LIVING

69

Does Life Seem Like One Long Busy Signal?

Not With Datumexx!

As an executive, you know that your telephone can be the most important part of your job. And you also know it can be your biggest headache.

We'd like you to meet the future of communications—THE DATUMEXX BI-COASTAL PHONE SYSTEM.

• • •

Let us surgically implant our tiny microchip in your brain, and you can say "Sayonara" to the inconvenience of conventional telephones. Yes, once our expert technicians have installed the Datumexx Bi-Coastal Phone System in your frontal lobe, you'll be able to reach whom you want, whenever you want, from wherever you want, *just by thinking of the number.*

No cords, no buttons, no clumsy receivers, no expensive monthly phone bills. Only a small incision above the left eyebrow.

And ask about our Time-Zone Equalizer, the option that eliminates the three-hour time difference between New York and Los Angeles!

The Datumexx Bi-Coastal Phone System. Because we feel that nothing should get in the way of a deal.

THE DATUMEXX BI-COASTAL PHONE SYSTEM
NOW AVAILABLE IN NEW YORK • LOS ANGELES • BOSTON • SAN FRANCISCO
More service areas coming soon

It could be <u>your</u> child saying...

"Come quick! Pop's on TV!"

...with the specialized training you'll receive from
The Man-On-The-Street Institute!

Out of work? Perhaps you've considered a career in television, but aren't sure how to break in. Well, at the Man-on-the-Street Institute, we'll prepare you for an entry-level position in broadcast television. That's right—at The Man-on-the-Street Institute, our instructors will train you to provide the hackneyed opinions and sentiments that local and network news reports are crying out for.

When you graduate, we'll find you jobs in the growing ranks of ordinary people who get their faces on the evening news.

You'll learn what to say about everything, from homicidal maniacs:

"He always seemed like a perfectly nice boy. Sure, he kept to himself a lot, but we're all shocked he would shoot that many people!"

To major sporting events:

"I'm telling you, we're going all the way this year!"

We'll teach you generic reactions to any natural catastrophe, such as "First, there was this, uh, like this blinding flash, and then sort of a terrific rumble." We even offer seminars in fielding tough questions ("Well, it tastes something like chicken") and impersonating the relative of a terrorist hostage—whether

THIS COULD BE YOU

WELL, THE SKY GOT PITCH BLACK, Y'KNOW, AND THEN EVERYTHING GOT REAL QUIET...

I FIGURE WE'RE JUST ONE OR TWO PLAYERS AWAY FROM A PENNANT!

THEY WERE SAUCER-SHAPED AND SILVERY--AND THEY HAD ALL THESE BLINKING LIGHTS...

it's Mom ("We can only pray that this horrible ordeal will end soon") or Uncle Lou ("Personally, I think we ought to nuke 'em").

Newscasts everywhere need people like you to state the obvious, so why keep your boring opinions to yourself? The Man-on-the-Street Institute will give you the confidence and know-how to comment on issues you're not familiar with, personalities you've never met, and events you never witnessed.

73

Write Us Today!
Don't settle for just saying "Hi, Mom" in the background!

THE MAN-ON-THE-STREET INSTITUTE
OF NORWALK, CONNECTICUT

APPROVED FOR VETERANS!

Leisure and Creativity Aids

Is Your Unconscious As Rich As It Should Be?

I F YOU'RE not using your unconscious enough, you're not using a Supercort.

The Supercort Unconscious...it's:

•**Rugged**—strong enough to influence all aspects of existence. No other major psychic construct comes close to its explanatory power.

•**Big**—contains up to 95 percent of everything you know and feel.

•**Lightweight**—goes everywhere you go.

The Supercort Unconscious comes with a personalized set of wishes, symbols, condensations, displacements, and projections. Talk about versatility! The Supercort has a thousand uses for waking and dream life, home and office. And it's indispensable for love, hate, creativity, even for recalling the lyrics of songs you haven't heard for years. With an unconscious from Supercort, every Freudian slip has a deep meaning!

No other unconscious so efficiently stores an unlimited number of childhood memories. Or lets you sleep so peacefully through most dreams without working. The Supercort conveniently converts unpleasant experiences into physical symptoms, and you don't have to lift a finger.

And for a limited time only, when you buy or lease a Supercort Unconscious, you'll also receive a *Supercort Preconscious*—for those times when you seek something more than obliviousness to, but less than full awareness of, what's really going on!

The Supercort Unconscious. Even when you're not thinking about it, it's thinking about you.

LISTEN TO WHAT OWNERS OF THE SUPERCORT UNCONSCIOUS ARE SAYING

"I used to wonder why I did things. Now I know."

Aaron Fejard
Norwalk, Ohio

"Before, I thought about everything I did. Now I let my Supercort Unconscious think for me....And I have more time for the things I really enjoy."

Barry O'Brian
Portsmouth, New Hampshire

Supercort UNCONSCIOUS

Enjoy life!

Well, it's easier said than done. For the anxious, the self-conscious, and the workaholic, having fun can be the hardest job of all.

Well, cheer up! The Feldman Fun Indicator takes the guesswork out of pleasure identification! Just place this handy little device anywhere there's pleasure potential and it lets you know the moment fun has been achieved, by exploding harmlessly in a hail of glitter and confetti while playing a recording of Kool and the Gang's "Celebrate!"

Now you *know* you're having fun!!

Use one any time you go out or when you're just self-amusing alone at home. With its colorful, musical burst of excitement, the Fun Indicator tells you it's time to turn from Type A into *Type A-OK!!!*

Only the Feldman Fun Indicator is capable of taking the sensitive atmospheric readings necessary to determine when actual fun occurs...signaling you and your friends to enjoy yourselves even when you're still completely miserable or preoccupied with your past.

So why the long faces, guys? C'mon, everybody, let's party! You only go around once! Transform that Where?-and-When? into a festive Here!-and-Now! and *get down.* Can you dig it?

Of course you can. The Fun Indicator. From Feldman. We know you can be spontaneous if you just plan ahead.

Available in convenient six-packs.

The **FELDMAN** *Fun Indicator!*

Have your fur coat...
and _wear_
it, too!

I belong to the ACLU. I give generously to the ASPCA. I even voted for Walter Mondale.

My politics are above reproach...but I happen to love fur.

And that's why I buy my garments from Mr. Pierre Peters. Every fur in his Eleganza Collection has been pre-trashed to insure guilt-free wearing pleasure. Where else can you choose from a tasteful selection of blood-stained mink, spat-upon ermine, ink-splattered sable, and slashed rabbit? Every garment looks just like it's already been violated by animal-rights activists.

You know, I wish I were strong enough to resist the temptation to drape myself in the skins of cruelly slaughtered, innocent animals...but I'm not. Now, with a Pierre Peters fur, everyone thinks I've already been victimized for my views—and that means I can wear fur proudly in public, with complete peace of mind.

What can I say? Buying an expensive fur with pieces of bubble gum already stuck on it gives me a good warm feeling.

And to me that's priceless.

The Eleganza Collection
by Mr. Pierre Peters

FINALLY, THE <u>ONE</u> SHOE FOR <u>ALL</u> THE EXERCISE I'M NOT GETTING!

In today's confusing world of athletic footwear, there's an expensive shoe for every sport and activity. But what if you don't exercise? Is there a reasonably priced shoe for you?

Clatt Industries introduces the Sloth, the shoe that takes all the guesswork out of what to wear when you want to avoid physical exertion of any kind.

This remarkable shoe, years in the making, has absolutely no cushioning or support. In no way does it conform to the shape of the human foot. Just slipping it on dramatically increases the odds of shock-related injuries to the bones, muscles, and tendons of the lower leg. In fact, a recent poll of leading podiatrists and sports-medicine experts concluded that attempting any physical activity in it will do irreparable damage to your feet. That's because the Sloth's patented Korrugated inner sole is engineered to cripple you almost immediately, whether you're not jogging, aerobicizing, or enjoying racquet sports.

The truth is, you can barely stand up in it.

The Sloth.

Until now, you couldn't find one shoe for the wide range of activities you didn't engage in.

One size doesn't fit anybody.

NO OTHER SHOE HAS ALL THESE FEATURES:

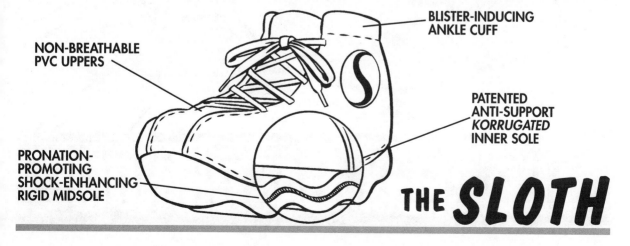

BLISTER-INDUCING ANKLE CUFF

NON-BREATHABLE PVC UPPERS

PATENTED ANTI-SUPPORT *KORRUGATED* INNER SOLE

PRONATION-PROMOTING SHOCK-ENHANCING RIGID MIDSOLE

THE *SLOTH*

WHEN YOU ALREADY HAVE EVERY KITCHEN APPLIANCE IN THE WORLD, YOU'RE READY FOR...

THE FELIX GASTRONOME

We searched the world over for the latest kitchen appliance, and we found lt for you in Italy. It's by far the most sophisticated, most advanced, most beautifully designed culinary addition imaginable to your gourmet kitchen environment. *The Felix Gastronome.*

STUNNING EUROPEAN DESIGN!

This handsomely crafted, superbly engineered appliance does for you what no juicer, no food processor, no espresso-, pasta-, or ice cream-maker could ever hope to do. With its full range of toasting levels, complete array of prongs, rotating diamond disk, hand-hammered copper infusion element, tempered steel rotary blade, and ceramic base, the Felix Gastronome is one of the world's finest examples of function-preemptive form.

No appliance in our experience displays as much versatility combined with such utility-free operation. And we know you'll appreciate the Gastronome's twin nozzle capacity, just one of the many features which prove that nonimplementation need not mean ostentation.

MONEY-BACK GUARANTEE!

The Felix Gastronome. We guarantee you that everything it doesn't do, it fails to do more expensively and with more European flair than any appliance you've ever owned.

Now, tell us—with all the costly kitchen appliances you already own that you never use, isn't it a relief to know there's one you can own—and neglect—without guilt?

The Felix Gastronome. If it did anything at all, we could never charge so much for it.

BORN UNDER THE SIGN OF PEPPERONI!

This budget-minded gourmet treat from Gusto combines two American favorites, astrology and pizza, in one scrumptious horoscope.

The Pizziac comes in twelve presliced sections, each corresponding to one of the sun signs and covered with a different heavenly topping (anchovy for Pisces, pepperoni for Cancer, and so on). Don't bother to ask, "What's your sign?" because you'll be able to tell by which piece of the astrological pie your guests go for! But before you bite into our crispy crust, tangy tomato sauce, and double-rich mozzarella, don't forget to look under each slice for a revealing message about the drives and energies that make up your essential character!

Pizziac is a terrific icebreaker for first dates, a stimulating conversation piece for parties, and just an all-around great way to delve into the mysteries of the human psyche and load up on cholesterol at the same time.

Once you've had your first slice of Pizziac, you'll realize that your Sun Sign is also your Fun Sign. We think you'll agree—it's one zesty zodiac!

When it comes to a Pizziac, we were all born under the sign of Gusto!

The PIZZIAC from Gusto

This Pot *NEVER NEEDS* Watching!

Thanks to PAGANO'S PERPETUAL PASTA

It's versatile, inexpensive, good-tasting, and good for you.

The only problem with pasta is that, to cook it, you have to boil water. And that can take more time than you have, whether you're watching the pot or not.

Unless you use Pagano's Perpetual Pasta. A single one-pound Starter Box contains an indefinite supply of the pasta of your choice. All you do is prepare Pagano's Perpetual Pasta the usual way, enjoy it, and remember to leave a little in the pot. Overnight, Pagano's Perpetual Pasta regenerates automatically, giving you a fresh pot of *al dente* pasta for your next meal. And it keeps regenerating, day after day.

No more pots to watch. No more linguini to drain. Just perfect pasta. Whether you want it or not. In fact, your original Starter Box of Pagano's will still be putting pasta on your table long after you're dead.

So use your noodle. As long as the noodle you're using is Pagano's Perpetual Pasta.

How much time do you waste getting halfway through an article before realizing you have no interest in it? Or eyeing those stacks of old unread magazines and wondering if there's something in them that could change your life? If the information explosion has blown up in your face and you know less than ever because there's so much to choose from, the choice for you is the Margell Media Compactor.

In the time it takes you just to read the table of contents in *US* magazine, the Media Compactor will convert a full load of printed matter into a stapled document tailored to your reading tastes and mentality.

READ LESS—ENJOY MORE!

There's no more flipping, skimming, or digging for relevant information. Just pack up to 25 pounds of newspapers, magazines, newsletters, research reports, junk mail, and books into the Input Bin. Then set the dial to your Zone of Interest—let's say Celebrity Profiles and Horoscopes—and hit the start button. Within a minute the Margell Media Compactor electronically scans the load (including advertisements) for celebrity features and astrological prognostications, lays them out, and reprints them in a uniform typeface on heavy stock.

START SAVING TIME AT ONCE!

Whether you set the dial for Mideast Policy or January White Sales, you get only what you need to read. The gist...without the grist.

So contact your local Margell dealer today and get right to the point...without all the pap.

The Media Compactor. What you don't want to know won't hurt you anymore.

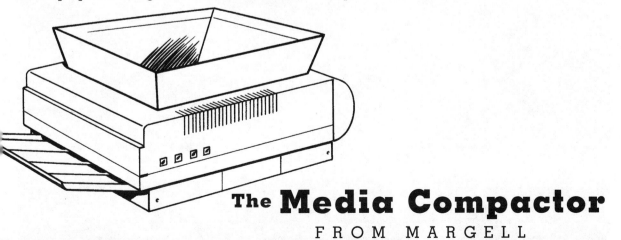

The **Media Compactor**
FROM MARGELL

Now On Videocassette!
THE WIDE WORLD OF EVERYTHING
PERHAPS THE ONLY DOCUMENTARY
YOU'LL EVER NEED TO WATCH!

Like most of us, you want to be well-informed, but reading is out of the question and, to be frank, most documentaries leave a little something to be desired.

That's why we've made *The Wide World of Everything* available on videocassette. It's the documentary that covers every subject known to man in a *single one-hour show*.

Join your host Walter Paulk, won't you, for an intimate look at people, places, ideas, issues, societies, old myths, new frontiers, and what-have-you, all of it narrated by Paulk's orotund tones to the accompaniment of a variety of impressive music.

Where conventional documentaries take a lot of your time to tell you more than you want to know about a single obscure issue that seldom affects your life, *The Wide World of Everything* superficially examines everything that could possibly matter: white flight, black markets, Gray Panthers, red scares, yellow rain, blue movies, corporate greenmail, Agent Orange... indeed, the whole spectrum of threats to our way of life.

The Wide World of Everything. Sixty minutes. One hour. And you'll never have to watch a documentary again.

*   *   *

Originally made possible in part by a grant from a big company, with additional funding provided by another big company, plus smaller amounts of money from smaller companies.

THE WIDE WORLD OF EVERYTHING

You'll see this man talking....

and this woman...

and then you'll see this man talking...

You'll even see Walter Paulk listening.

Then you'll see this man talking again!

91

Index

acting,out, neurotic, 13
activities not engaged in, wide range of, 83
ambitions, unrealistic, 68
an arm and a leg: *see* world, increasingly
   litigious
ancient family conflict, deepening of, 18
annoying traces of style, elimination of, 67

behavior, quality-timer, 38
bran, resistance to, 54
bric-a-brac, removal of, 53
brunches, bad, detection of, devices
   for the, 51

caring, deep interpersonal, 13
childhood inequalities, eradication of, 40-41
communication obfuscators: *see* verbal
   representations
conflict, intrapsychic, 21
conversation, trivial, 22-23
counsel, legal, access to inexpensive, 33

early promise, squandering of, 65
egos, other people's, 24
emotional distance, measurement of, 19
emotion-reduction technology, 37
employers, unique smell of, 63
events, mental, accurate recording of, 69
everything that could possibly matter, 90-91
exertion, physical, avoidance of, 82-83
existence, revision of, 30-31

facial features, infantile, improvement of, 44
family life, wrenching emotional reality of, 18
feelings, hurt, 14-15
fiction and nonfiction, concentrated
   versions of, 67
first marriages: *see* memories and sensations

food conveyance, airline, 55
form, function-preemptive, 85
funding, additional, 91
furs, guilt-free wearing of, 81

gentrification prediction, 42-43
gestures, socially desirable, 23
gossip, grief, and grievances, normally
   associated with family contact, 18
gourmet treats, budget-minded, 86
guilt, due to ownership of costly kitchen
   appliances, relief of, 85

hopes, dashed, 69

idle teenagers, large concentrations of, 39
impressive music, a variety of, 91
incentives, token, 43
information, explosion of, 89
information, minimal residue of, 67
ingestion aids: *see* food conveyance
innocent animals, cruelly slaughtered,
   skins of, 81
insecure, protection for the, 24
intruders, annihilation of, 57
involvement, passionate, 13

jargon stylings, personalized, 26-27

knickknacks, ill-advised purchases of, 53

life's disappointments, obsessive monologues
   about, 11
lonely nights, turning of into festive
   occasions, 10-11
literary allusions, namby-pamby, 26

Richard Rosen is the author of *Psychobabble* and three mystery novels, including the Edgar Award-winning *Strike Three You're Dead*. His work in television comedy as a writer and performer spans PBS (*The Generic News*), *Saturday Night Live*, and HBO's *Not Necessarily the News*. He is the cocreator and costar of HBO's *News to Us*. He lives in New York City with his family.

Steve Vance is a designer, illustrator, and sometime writer. His work has appeared on or in countless album covers, ad campaigns, magazines, greeting cards, posters, and comic books. He coauthored, with Matt Groening, the recent book *The Postcards That Ate My Brain*. He and his wife have their own design studio, Artropolis, in Los Angeles.